GONE SELF STORM

Gone Self Storm

Harry Clifton

WAKE FOREST UNIVERSITY PRESS

First North American edition

Published in Britain and Ireland by Bloodaxe Books Ltd.

For permission, write to

Wake Forest University Press

Post Office Box 7333

Winston-Salem, NC 27109

WFUPRESS.WFU.EDU

ISBN 978-1-943667-06-2 (paperback)

LCCN 2022948462

Designed and typeset by

Nathan Moehlmann,

Goosepen Studio & Press.

Cover Image: *Moonlight, Wood Island Light*, 1894

(Winslow Homer, 1836–1910), oil on canvas.

Gift of George A. Hearn, in memory of Arthur Hoppock Hearn, 1911.

Metropolitan Museum of Art, 11.116.2.

Publication of this book was made possible

by generous support from the Boyle Family Fund.

GONE SELF STORM

Acknowledgments

Acknowledgments are due to the editors of the following publications in which some of these poems first appeared: *Channel, Irish Pages, The Irish Times, Manhattan Review, Poetry Ireland Review, The North, The Poetry Review, Wild Fish* (Cambridge), *The Yellow Nib*, and *Shine On: Irish Writers for Shine* (Dedalus Press, 2011). "The Has-beens" was written in response to a commission for the Centenary of the first publication of James Joyce's *Ulysses*.

Contents

PART ONE

i.m. Dorothy Francesca Brandon Clifton, 1928–2019

11	A Ship Came from Valparaiso
12	Chile
14	To the Engineer Herbert Ashe
16	Sin-eater
17	Neruda
19	Rapa Nui
20	The Widow Transitito
21	Stepmother
23	Woman's Home Companion
24	The Zeal of the Convert
26	What a Boy Should Know
27	Atacama Clothes-dump
28	Mother and Son
30	Whatever It Is
31	A Woman Drives Across Ireland
33	A House Called Stormy Weather
35	The Aching Void
37	Goodnight Antofagasta
39	White City

PART TWO

43	Glasnevin Clay
46	Gainor Crist
48	The Has-beens
50	Going Feral
51	Alice
53	Staten Island Ferry

54 Harvard Yard

55 The Fur Trade

57 The Gig with the Golden Microphone

59 On Ventry Strand

60 Amergin

62 Nafooey

64 The Salmon Cages

66 Radio Silence

67 After the Barbarians

69 Inscape

PART THREE
i.m. Mary Bridget McKavanagh Madden, 1925–2014

75 The Felling

79 In Brontë Country

80 Spinsters

82 Notes for a Townland

83 Honesty

84 The Decoys

85 The Sweep

86 Jericho

88 The Place of the Stonings

89 The Pure Source

91 Diatomite

92 The Ulster Cycle

94 Toome

96 Germinal

98 Praeger

99 The Earliest Breakfast in Northern Ireland

100 At the Grave of Seamus Heaney

PART ONE

The moon
Is at the mast-head and the past is dead.
Her mind will never speak to me again.

Wallace Stevens

A SHIP CAME FROM VALPARAISO

Thainig long o Valparaiso
Pádraig de Brún

I was conceived, the story goes,
On a Dutch tramp steamer
Plowing the Magellan Straits
Halfway to Buenos Aires.

There was one passenger,
Diabetic. Every day,
Daddy, with an insulin shot,
Went below to keep him alive.

Behind lay the ghosts of the Andes,
Ireland ahead. In between,
A city of dreams,
Concepción ... There put in,

For water, sex, fresh food,
The bad eggs and the good —
And one wild night
Could change a life forever.

He would die, be buried at sea,
That man, with all his knowledge.
No third parties please
To love on the high seas.

And the name of the ship
Would be given me, the firstborn,
Sailing north, out of waters
I never cease to explore.

CHILE

If I go there, it will be in my own time —
And what will I find there? Things foresuffered

From childhood, dumped like baggage on a runway,
Such the hurry of Mother and Father to leave.

A language all conditionals, subjunctives
In a land of might-have-been, where the cloudscapes thicken

Like myth, on the hiddenness of the Andes,
And it rains but once a year, in the far, far north,

In the space before I was born, the oldest space on earth
Where you can see too far for your own good

And emptiness dogs you like a shadow, through the salt-flats
And the foothills, far into Bolivia,

And the sky is impossibly blue, or call it the void.
And the waves of Mejillones, self-destroyed,

Break endlessly off the Pacific… Ante-natal,
Father swims, and Mother, among prehistoric life-forms,

In the amniotic warmth. I have yet to be born,
To come into the knowledge of myself and go back home

To the locus of pure suffering, before history,
Picking up baggage along the runway,

Keeping the orphan in me loved, and the salt-mine worker fed,
Claiming, as birthright, all that was left unsaid.

TO THE ENGINEER HERBERT ASHE

In his lifetime, he suffered from unreality

Jorge Luis Borges

He was sent up-country
Ignorant of the language,
With a radio, a cache of books
For company.
                  There were mountains
Out of this world, and lakes
Of white saltpeter, totally dead.
Moonscape. Frightening clarity.
Metaphysical dread.
Sunsets through the pristine air
Draining heat off the desert.
Coldness like a pistol shot
In the next room, on the wooden stair—
A suicide? No one there…

Once a week, the train came through—
Great flanges dripping snow.
A sack of victuals, a letter or two.
As for the books—too civilized, sick,
And night came on too quick.
He put them aside and rhapsodized,
Pathos draining through his rhymes
Like an old school primer.
Tried the radio. Stadium roar
From another lifetime—
Somewhere, a goal being scored…

So much for beauty, the sublime.
So much, with the help of lost weekends,
For the passing of time,
The sleeping-off of drink and demons,
Watched by a bowler-hatted
Crew of Indians...
                    Year on year
A woman waited, down at the coast.
One day, she would take him out of there—
The waterless deserts
And the deserted waters—
Void on void, as man, as wife,
To married bliss, an afterlife
Of haunted sons and daughters.

SIN-EATER

They say, if you marry beneath yourself
It teaches you everything. Daddy, I watch you
Go down in the world, as reality
Rises to meet you…. A girl off the shelf,

A desert behind her, alcohol, orphanhood.
You explain to her about history, about home.
She tells you about emptiness, the void.
She will stand for your anthem. You will swim

Too gingerly, in the cold of her ocean,
Out of your element… Mother, rescue him
Quick, from the shadow electric, in slow motion —
Manta ray, beneath the glass-bottomed boat

Of marriage, where the honeymooners float…
Such a union should produce, at most,
One eater of sin, to feast on both your love-letters,
Share your grave, like an expiated ghost.

NERUDA

You were given a country
To play with. A mountain range,
The thousand-mile-long fault-line
Of the Andes. Anteworlds,
A racket of mating-calls
Before the Fall, a tropical zoo
To come back to. Chile
Of course, the old green Eden
Of Temuco, giant butterflies
And bird-cries out of a childhood
Dank and paradisal
As Connemara...
                    So it is
I read in you the lives of the saints
Where waywardness, excess,
Are each man's way of saying yes
To creation... Settings-out
Again and again, to the theatres
Of action, disillusion—
Russia, Spain. Mass rallies,
Goings into hiding. Escape
Across the passes, to an afterlife
Torn between platform
And people. Now, to come back
To the grain, the grape,
Tomato, wine, the crumb of bread,

The humble, the unsaid,

                    is my America
Here instead. The Isla Negra
Of Connemara, where the Atlantic,
The Pacific, are one and the same
And everyone reads from the very first page,
The mother tongue is learned again,
The child-self stumbled upon
By the beachcomber, in old age.

RAPA NUI

(Easter Island)

I go there, once in a while,
To remind myself where I came from.
A dumping-ground of archetypes

Dead-eyed, looking out
On the heyday of willpower,
Intelligence that can only go so far.

Somebody with an Irish name
Once claimed it for a nation,
Forgot it again, for a hundred years,

The great Self, outstaring
Its manifestations—land and sea,
War and history—east to the Corderillas,

Chile, and the rising sun
Of Ballantyne and Stevenson.
Once, I would have called it paradise,

Not now ... Accumulated fact,
Catastrophe in disguise.
The less I know, the wiser I am

Approaching it, abandoning it
Like an island, or a dream
Awakened from, bereft,

Where something bad once happened
I need never go back to,
Never having left.

THE WIDOW TRANSITITO

We keep coming back, the widow and I,
To knock on each other's door
With our tale of abandonment, life of wanderings,
Dark pre-history…
                     Unprovided for
Didn't she start some kind of boarding-house,
Follow me north, on the *Reina del Mar,*
My lady of sorrows? Now she is watching me,
Through a window in greater London,
The widow, as I cast about
In her garden of long grass, her junkyard of Eden,
For a lever, a latch-key, some way in
To the first address, and the shame of origin.

Death means nothing between us. Ever-living,
Seeing each other, face on face
Ancestral, mirrored in the double-glaze
Of time and space….
                     I have circled back
Through all these years, to bring it home to her—
The ocean of loneliness, the afterglow
Of the Americas, once long ago.
Be not afraid, I say to her. Admit me, your godson.
We have been alone too long,
The pair of us, and been turned away
From too many doors, for the world to be anything
Better than common lodging
Between us now, who have only each other.

STEPMOTHER

You were drafted in
At the moment of conception,
Filling an empty space—
And I learned to call you Mother.

"Your coming into the world
Was agony, but I loved you ..."
You quoted, a little too naturally,
From the book of parenthood.

Not that I disliked you
Or you me. But it seemed
The ship that stranded you here
Had sunk before birth.

You would never get back, now,
To the first place. Letters
Came, stamped with the mystical birds
Of a non-existent country

I pasted into the Here and Now.
Every morning, dressing me
You shook with sobs, at ten by the clock.
I watched, and said nothing.

Later, I learned your history.
A man you called great
Had rescued you, like God the Father,
And set you up, in house and home.

You nailed your wedding dress
To the wall, and worshipped it
Like marriage. You baked bread
From stones of the desert

On which I quietly fed.
When the time came
For truth-telling, good behavior
Had made you the liar you are.

That I was motherless
No one told me. That your emptiness
Was holy, a lifetime in the desert,
I would find out by myself.

WOMAN'S HOME COMPANION

Daddy, on his big black
Motorbike, roars off
Into the fifties. Mother
Comes upstairs, to dress me.

"Mammy, why are you crying?"
"Oh, because Daddy
Won't eat his breakfast..."
Remembering, after all these years,

I come up behind them
Gently now, and take her
By the waist, and feel it,
Their silent weeping

All of them, as the heads,
The hair scraped back
For daily duty, lean against me
In their lonely millions.

THE ZEAL OF THE CONVERT

1

Born again, before irony
Or civilization, I feel myself
Held once more by a hand.

We are going somewhere,
Mother and I. All Hallows night—
The roar of trees, the space debris

Of old cosmogonies
In the dark... And a hand,
Her hand. The high road

If I remember, to the church
At Kilmacud, whether
Catholic or Church of Ireland

Now it hardly matters—
Baptized in both, belonging to neither,
The stepson and the mother.

2

The days of the dead are upon us,
The high road to Kilmacud
Our *via negativa*.

The weeping has stopped,
The browbeaten silence
At the kitchen table,

Doors being slammed, uneaten food.
The Jesuit has gone away.
At last you have seen the light of day.

And here we are, on the autumn road
Where witches, ghosts are abroad,
Unchristened, unmentioned,

About whom I do not ask,
Wearing, as we do ourselves,
Faith like a Halloween mask.

3

You, who are all I know of religion,
Bringer of the one true void
Into the dwelling-place,

Good mother, good wife,
Sworn at last to eternal life,
I alone, with the eye of a stepchild,

See, behind genuflectings, gongs,
The zeal of the convert
Who never belongs.

The masks are all off, now,
The churches empty. Civilization,
Irony, cannot save us.

Supernatural friends,
Soul-wanderers, there we go
In darkness, holding hands.

WHAT A BOY SHOULD KNOW

Spring was everywhere, Ireland on show
Not only to itself, but to the world.
There were books now "suitable for girls"
And for the likes of me *What a Boy Should Know*.

There were May Devotions, and the sacred word
Novena. Hunched forms, Mother and I,
The doomed protectress, under the Virgin's eye
All-seeing…. When I think of it, now, the jailbirds

And the judges we became, my mind goes back
Two generations, to a corrugated shack
Beside the Pacific, and a woman who waits

In nothing but a medal and a myth
For salt-mine workers, lone expatriates
In from the cold, to get it over with.

ATACAMA CLOTHES-DUMP

Add to it cast-offs, hand-me-downs
From the postwar years—my christening gown,

My llama fleeced, vicuna shorn
To clothe me, from the land before birth,

For the nakedness of my going forth
In the Age of Aquarius, somewhere far to the north—

My cheesecloth, paisley, corduroy,
The disco thump, and the brief orgasmic cry

Dumped in the desert, wheeled above in the sky,
Picked among, by a pueblo Indian

Wise to the seven ages of man,
The biodegradable selves, hung out to dry

From Chuqui to Calama, Ollague
To Antofagasta, where my vanities lie.

MOTHER AND SON

The high skylit room
He kept to, in his final phase,
Is a dustbowl of dreams.
I stand in metaphysical space

On the top rung of a ladder
And think generations —
My head in his attic,
My place among the nations.

And the small voice
At the foot of the family tree
I threaten to fall out of
Is Mother, cautioning me.

"Do not, my son, overbalance
Into the higher life.
The parable of the talents
Was always a one-off...."

And it trembles, his drawbridge
On family, on marriage,
History come to no good end,
The whole idea of Ireland....

"Take what you need, my son,
From the dust and ashes
Of abstraction, lightning flashes —
But remember, life goes on."

His empty desk, tobacco smell,
His ladder and trap-
Door—I hang there still—
As the voice drifts up.

WHATEVER IT IS

You look so old, Harry. And you've put on weight
But your face is thin. And your hair—
Remember how I used to brush it at the parting?

You hated that. But you still have good teeth
I'm glad to see. And the delicate hands
That run in our family. And the color-blindness

That came down my side, naturally, though only in the men.
Thank you, by the way, for not revealing me
In print. It would have brought back everything.

Do you see your brothers these days? Or your cousins?
I refrain from mentioning children
Except to ask you, Harry, do you ever notice

How we seem to be endlessly clearing our throats,
You and I, and nothing coming out,
And would they inherit it, do you think? Whatever it is.

A WOMAN DRIVES ACROSS IRELAND

The deacon must have been sixty, and the priest
Of an age with myself, was old enough
To have seen through everything, even love—
He sighed, as if to say "Ite, Missa Est"
And then die happy. Yes, it was over now
For a whole generation, rising to their feet
To bless themselves.... The church on Francis Street
Meant nothing anymore. I was driving west

That Sunday morning, with the traffic light
And all my life behind me ... children, sex,
The man who brought me here. I could relax
Without the radio, or the conversational flights
I knew by heart—interferences
On the invisible ether. I was free at last
To switch them off and trust my own experience.
I was closing a house that belonged to all our past.

A student I picked up, beyond Maynooth,
Lit into me at once with "Are you Saved?
Have you made your peace with God? Because Antichrist
Is everywhere, and the brethren are divided
In this land...." As if to confirm a truth
The Bord na Móna stacks and the vaulted naves
Of Catholic churches loomed. Alone, obsessed,
I left her, like a daughter I had lost.

Athlone went by in a dream, and Ballinasloe—
The barracks, the asylum. Ireland's energies
Pent behind brickwork twice the height of a man.
Ahead of me, container trucks rolled on

To their eternal Monday mornings, and a breeze,
Where the scarp descended, started to blow
From the cold Atlantic. Still, I was half in love
With the life I had married into, and risen above.

A woman flagged me down, near Athenry
With an ancient tale that could have been my own—
Her children left behind, her man disowned
In a fit of panic. "What else could I do?"
She laughed hysterically, began to cry.
"The drunken bastard beat me black and blue
But never again…." I dropped her at Oranmore.
I had been that road a hundred times before

And gone back home…. I knew the lie of the land,
The changes of emotion, shifts of gear,
The lie of marriage, like the back of my hand,
The twisted roads that led, like lines of fate,
Through Galway, Oughterard, the Western Gate,
Deeper into the mountains, all those years
I lived again, as I drove forever nearer
An empty house that was filling up with sand.

Above the Inagh valley, I stopped my car
Out of sheer wonderment, at how far
I had come, and how much I had survived.
I thought of all the lives I might have lived
Instead of choosing Ireland, and one man.
A million grassblades, whispering in the breeze,
Reminded me I was no one, and the peace
Felt huge inside me, as the night came on.

A HOUSE CALLED
STORMY WEATHER

To paint from memory of gone self storm
John Keats

I heard enough of the sea
To remember it forever.
In the pause between the waves
The sound of a little river
Chattering seaward, over its stones—
I feel it now, in my bones....

There was time to draw breath
Before the next crash,
And hear, in the silent interval,
The chimney-drip in the ashes,
Safe as I was in the nights, the days,
The man-made space

Of children and begetters.
And when the wind rose,
In a rattle of green shutters
That would never properly close,
Sleep banged back on itself
But nothing fell off the shelf,

The little things, against the storm,
Stood firm, their essence
Inexhaustible, in the house
Of being, where nothing ever lessens
Either side of death—
A house called Stormy Weather

Named for a song, another age
Of smoke and jazz, so long ago
The moment of love
That made me I will never know,
Lying here, in the after-peace
Between two ancestries,

Sleeping in the ruins,
In an autumn of spring tides,
The ruins of reality
Where everyone has died
And everyone lives forever,
Sleeping open-eyed,

Hearing the little river
Chattering seaward, over its stones,
The chimney-drip on the ashen floor—
I feel it in my bones—
The moment's silence, then the roar
Of pure becoming, gone self storm

That bends but never breaks
The non-existent glass,
The knick-knacks and the paperbacks,
The indestructible open house
Of dead and living, frozen time,
And I who call it home.

THE ACHING VOID

A child sits, reading a book.
And suddenly, old age
Overtakes her. Absently
She reaches out

For the dog turned to dust
Who stood between her
And lovelessness.
                 Listen—
Is that the sea in the distance?

Certainly the voices—
If voices are still calling her,
If voices ever called her—
Are bird-cries now, drowned out.

And the book? Which book
Is she still stuck in the middle of?
Seventy years flew by
Like a dream—

White hair. And a gull-scream
Right through everything
In between. *Tropical summer—*
Father drank from a demijohn

In a shed at the end of the earth.
Mother, you see, was a good-time girl.
And then one day, a nice man came
And took me away…

Back to front, upside down,
Inside out, the book of the years.
Her hand reaches out
And the dog appears.

GOODNIGHT ANTOFAGASTA

Tokyo Rose and Vera Lynn,
Ocean voices on the wind,
War going on all over the world
And this one area of the Pacific
Empty, where nothing was happening
But the dustbowl of San Pedro
To the north, the wind from the Andes
Cold off the Atacama
After dark, on the bars, the honky-tonks—
Antofagasta … And a girl-child
Listening, after midnight, to the bulletins
Coming through, in an English voice—
The tonnages of shipping sunk,
The carnage at the fronts—a level voice,
Emotionless, saying *Goodnight Antofagasta*
And a violin playing.
                  Then silence
Wide as the Pacific, turning its blind eye
On wartime. Adoring, after its fashion,
The infinities … Radio silence, or the hiss
And crump of rollers coming ashore
On the beach at Mejillones further north
Where no one would ever invade
For what did the Germans care, or the Japanese
For here, which was nowhere? Only a space,
A wide Pacific space, that people
Disappeared into, and they called it death,
The authorities.
                And to lay her down

Now, on this side of the earth
In her grave-clothes, carefully chosen
For hiddenness, whose one desire,
Having had us, was to leave us behind—
A voice among voices on the wind...
Goodnight Antofagasta the solo violin plays
And it's time for closure. For a moment
I see it, a sweep of ocean
No one knows, the islands uninhabited
For there is nothing there worth fighting for,
And the silence absolute, for there are no ears
To hear it, and the bird has flown,
The austral bird and the bird of the soul,
Unknowable, unknown.

WHITE CITY

White city, to the south of anywhere—
Forget the equator and the double hemispheres,

You have been there already. Childhood and death
Prefigured it, middle age made it myth,

And every visit there was a traveling back
To the ante-natal. A casino for luck

And surreys drawing up, in the small hours,
To the disorderly houses. And the enormous flowers

With polysyllabic names and powerful scent
Not even the sea could kill. And so it went,

The story and the fable, yours my friend—
The wandering women and the time without an end.

Before you were ever thought of, it was there—
White city, to the south of anywhere.

PART TWO

GLASNEVIN CLAY

1. *The Gravediggers*

Three of them slaking thirst, this Saturday
In the back-bar of the gravediggers' pub—
A black and lightless realm, where to drink is to pray
Not to a soul in a mirror, a cigarette stub,

But to the millions gone before,
The city of the dead, on this side of town,
Among whom Harry Clifton, Margaret Doran
Somewhere out of space-time, overgrown…

But they are easy with it. What they have to do
Is nothing, as it has always been—
The white Glasnevin clay, and the vertigo

Of half a century, that stands between
Me staring in, with the eyes of an orphaned child,
And these ones sipping bitter, sipping mild.

2. *Harry Cooling Clifton 1870–1956*

Strange it will be when everyone's ashes
Scatter themselves on the breeze, and days like this
No longer exist, and people like ourselves
So lonely for the past, in terror of the future
Call out to each other, on the avenues,
In the alleyways, of the city of the dead,
Having found it at last, the little site
Of crying and lamentation, yours for mine

And mine for yours, in forests of marble, stone
Collapsed on themselves, projecting a shadow
At the very least … No afterlife,
Forget about that. But still, a here and now
Where the living like ourselves, who come here once
In any life, to put each other down,
Can meet the stranger on an equal ground,
The last of men, whom loneliness has left
Undead, all-knowing, wise to who lies where.

3. *Margaret Doran 1893–1983*

Who stood between the Church
And true religion.

Who declared war on the Irish State
And knelt in the kitchen

At the hour of execution,
The silenced shout.

Who wore conviction
Like a hairshirt, inside out,

And the leather coat
Of revolution, and the cigarette,

Until the babies came,
The wrong state, the church of shame.

Who gave her body to Trinity College
And her soul to Rome —

Afloat in the dissecting room
Of carnal knowledge,

Safe in Kingdom Come,
With her pure sonata, Gaelic poem

Inscribed by Douglas Hyde,
Her brokenness, her bouts of pride

Whose city went up in flames,
Who vanishes, with the other names,

As I do, as I will,
Bitter knowledge, bitter pill,

Filling in time, Glasnevin clay,
Between now and death,

Tomorrow and yesterday,
Tidying up the myth.

GAINOR CRIST

Darragh O'Connell 1952–2018

Who the hell was Gainor Crist
You and I once asked.
Was he a genius? An also-ran?
Was he the Ginger Man

Swanning about Dublin in tweeds,
Frequenting the usual bars,
Affecting art, in the lost years
After the War, on a trail that leads

Us both to a time before birth
Where Nano Reid, in drafty digs,
Paints a man naked, stretched at her hearth,
An orange between his legs,

And Harry Kernoff, debonair,
And minor cubists, here and there,
Deconstruct and recreate
The birth of the Irish Free State....

A city attaches itself to his name—
Whole summers, before we were born,
Gone like the sound of the Dublin foghorn
Or the rumor he became.

Did he not die, as word would have it,
Drunk and penniless in Spain
A year out of Dublin, never seen again?
There are people like that,

Famous for being unknown,
Gone south, like Gainor Crist
Or you, dear friend, whose mystery
Will some day be my own.

THE HAS-BEENS

David Marcus 1924–2009

You who managed your decline
So beautifully, who withdrew
At just the right time—
Or was it luck?—from working the rooms
For talent, seeing the galleys through,
Please, could you help me manage mine?

Crippled with shyness, see me climb
Blind stairs, through the seventies,
To your high view over the Liffey.
Coat-rack, desk, linoleum—
This, the engine-room
Of reputations, literary heaven ...

"You're not married? That's good—
No dependents. Take a look
At the grey desolation outside.
I, too, am writing a book,
Not art, mind you, I'm through with that,
Just pure commercial tat."

Below in the Scotch House, on the rocks,
A lost generation
Stopped its watches. Cattle-shed, docks,
The "specter of emigration"—
If anyone so much as blinked
In that Berkeleyan think-space

Of Ireland, it would all fall through,
The sawdust floor, the national dream,
The *esse est percipi*
Of Seán Lemass's tidal shipping
Sold down the river, unredeemed
Since Nineteen Twenty-two....

"A word of advice. Stay clear
Of the fool's paradise
Of life in here.
Even the walls have ears and eyes.
You will stop writing. You will disappear
In the depths of the years...."

For Heaven's sake, can that be you
At the intersection
Decades later, as the decals change
And half of Ireland surges through
To its next re-incarnation?
Drooling, self-estranged,

Who once were cruel to be kind,
Do you recognize me
At fifty, a *protégé*
Thrown to the wolves, who takes your hand
On this, our desolate traffic-island,
Sped-through, left behind?

GOING FERAL

Only here, with a pack of starving hounds
In a tenement room or a patch of public ground

She and all the creatures learnt to share,
Did the humans, telling her she was not all there,

Abandon her forever or a while
To wander the forest of cities, like a child

Suckled on wolf's milk, smelling of dog,
Unable to defend herself, or beg

In a common language. Knowing the Word
But no grammar. Panting in surds

At the packs of the concerned—the half-sisters,
Half-brothers, cloned from the masters,

Finding her where they left her, curled
In the forgotten corner of a lost, unfallen world.

ALICE

(Khao I Dang 1981)

And then there was Alice, who was always giving,
Always living out of her better self,
In the long ago and far away
Where millions sat in camps, and the air was rank
With hanging fire. The No Man's Land
Called Khao I Dang, Panatnikom, Nong Khai
Where she pulled up sleeves and regally held sway,
Our sister of mercy…. Monsoon puddles shrank
To an iron stagnation. Time stood still
In the laterite distance, on the disputed hills,
As a water-truck, between hutments,
Sprayed its fantail of drops in the dust,
And the Chinese, the Khmer,
Had their beards plucked, hair by hair —
All of them bellboys now, in the Middle West.

It was the tree of the knowledge of good and evil —
No one was innocent. Only Alice,
Black-marketed in gold and tetracycline,
Boa constrictor skins, Laotian weed,
Was always clean….

              Herself and her baked breads,
The miracle of stone-ground flour
Found somewhere, eaten as loaves and fishes,
The meals for so many, and the impossible dishes
Conjured out of nothing. Dust and heat,
A far-off summer, high on the lost exaltations
Of *caritas*, relevance… Whiplash antennae
Blurting into life on the back seat,
Emergency cases, calls for blood donation.

Alice, the last of us now without power or money—
Is she still there,
Packed in her own dry ice
Like purity, fluent at last in Khmer,
Passed over by history, a wave beneath which flows
The unresisting algae of her red Irish hair?

STATEN ISLAND FERRY

Martin Folan 1955–2014

Years before the ferry, O those lights,
Those multicolored lights of the filling-station
Opposite King's Inns, in the Dublin night.
"That," you told me, "is an installation—

Realer than reality...." And to prove it
In you moved for years, and lived above it,
Steering cars in darkness just for fun
Inside a locked garage, with the headlights on.

Years later, on the ferry "People here
Are ghosts ..." you said, as the pair of us crossed
To the capital city of wealth and happiness,

Work and death, "... except for what they wear."
Dublin behind us, nothing up ahead
But coroner's evidence, what the critics said.

HARVARD YARD

My age was over and my generation gone

Czesław Miłosz

How lonely a place
It feels already, Harvard Yard
Since the eighties.... Adams House

Where Heaney roomed, when Bishop
Threw in the towel
Like Paz, like Robert Lowell—

Not to mention Dexter Gate
Enter and grow wise
Where Walcott, Brodsky, dollar-bait,

Miłosz down from Grizzly Peak,
Half of Europe behind him
Dying to speak,

Have handed back their postern key
To the lost, the liberal space
Of the eighteenth century.

Stock unsold on Grolier shelves—
And the Widener, the Lamont,
Putting up a civilized front

As the shamed democracies
Die from the top, like trees
Transplanted here, in the sandy Yard

Of Harvard, taking root
Too shallowly, in girls, semesters,
Privilege, to bear fruit.

THE FUR TRADE

Derek Mahon 1941–2020

They say it built New York.
A little man, in a sweatshop
Off Canal, inscribes his handiwork

"Rabbi" for "Rabbit"
Lining your winter astrakhan.
As is your habit,

After some trouble
With an uptown waiter
You leave it once again on the table,

Stalk off, into the Broadway lights.
An hour later, the call comes
"My hat…" as I was afraid it might.

For the price of a tip
I can have it back
On Eighty-ninth, from a rubbish-skip.

They are unsentimental, you see,
About things like poetry,
The Americans. Rabbit or rabbi,

The place for a literary man
Is by the kitchen, or the Gents,
Beneath the extractor fan.

Anyway, here it is.
May it keep your ears warm
Where the poetry biz

Like the ICA, is colder
Than Hudson Bay, and luxury trades
Like ours, are fool's gold

Beaten into art,
Boxed into chocolates, dried into flowers
For money by the hard of heart,

The Stuyvesants, the Vanderbilts,
Far from the sweatshop of the word,
The rabbit's cry unheard,

The whole, obscurely felt
Catastrophe of the soul, on which
Fifth Avenue is built.

THE GIG WITH THE GOLDEN MICROPHONE

Graham Bond 1937–1974

London without you is re-inventing itself
Like a jazz musician. Another spring
Atonal with birdnotes, and the promise of sex—
So Graham, wake from the dead and do your thing
On Hammond organ, alto sax,
And leave your linctus bottles on the shelf

Where they belong, in the Age of Addictions.
This is posterity—to be clear-headed,
Orchestrating the music of chances
You blew in a lifetime. Send us your benediction,
Potbellied magus, fair game
For loansharks, dealers, wives on maintenance—
You went for a walk one day, and they found you dead.

It is a long time now, since Nineteen Seventy-four.
Terrible how the world forgets, how the doors
Of the Brixton tube you flung yourself under
Open and close, and the ceaseless millions shuttle,
Dormant, mute, between brake and throttle.
Terrible the lost chord, in the traffic thunder.

Blood was washed from the sleepers. Life went on—
Another age, another sound.
If you came back now, to hang around
Finsbury Park, all would be lights and clocks,
White magic, the Seven Sisters Road
Policed against streetwalkers, the mortar and bricks
Through which Johnny Rotten exploded.

If you came back now, it would not be too late
For Ladbroke Grove, or Notting Hill Gate
To remember you. As for the rest,
All over London the players, the brilliant ghosts,
Have done themselves to death,
Demoralized…. When it all comes together,

As one day it will do, Graham, show us a sign—
The stigmata of your healed veins
In the purifying waters of Shannon, or of Ganges,
Your victories on the astral plane
Against the musical warlocks, with their black arts.
"There is no death, there are only changes,"

You used to say, to whoever would pick up the tab.
Klooks Kleek, Flamingo, the old Marquee
Are gone forever. Climb in the cab
With your real instruments, soon it will be dawn
And the gig with the golden microphone
Waits for a New Age, in the druid hub
Of England, where your ashes have been sown.

ON VENTRY STRAND

These children ... they are trying, I believe,
To speak the tongue of their ancestors. Practicing
On the likes of me. *An bhfuil aon Gaeilge agat?*
Conas a tá tú? Interrupting ballgames

And flirtations, buttonholing me,
A perfect stranger. Children, I want to say,
I am the soul of the universe — go away!
I crawled from Ventry surf the day before Christ

Or how many billion years, by human reckoning.
Older, anyway, than the reflections
Of heroes on horseback, as the tide withdraws
And sweeps the hoofprints clear,...
                                        Some terrible teacher

Out of childhood calls them together.
Tea and separate dormitories. Form lines.
I pick up a scallop shell. At Compostela
They would call it pilgrimage. The Blaskets

In the distance, so many times evoked
They need no language. Please now, leave me alone,
I know the place-names, history. My middens
Have yet to be found (I add to them this scallop)

And the blue-green water, the constellations
After dark, the wrecker's moon and the tides
Are all inside me, who was put ashore
To walk this way, before and after Ireland.

AMERGIN

(for Paddy Bushe and Fíona de Buis)

Hispanic in origin, like myself,
Legend has it he came ashore
With the Milesians, whoever they were,
From Hy Brasil, the Atlantic shelf,
Galicia maybe—somewhere between
Imaginary mists on the Bay of Kenmare
And real-time Cahirciveen.

His airy epigraph *I am wind*
Off the sea about all I know,
But just enough, on Waterville strand
From Chaplin's bronze to the Butler Arms,
Watching the solstice come and go,
To ward off Ireland like a charm
And keep me from all harm.

The Skelligs, where the angry gods
At the edge of the world, like Star Wars,
Bat each other out of the clouds,
Lie westward... Saint John's fires
Smoke lazily, on Hog and Bolus Heads,
And the hungover, in the village bars,
Forget where they left their cars

After the night of revelry,
Midsummer.... And the breaking sea,
The vague, ambiguous force,
The living salt, the birth of nations
Out of dark immensity
Unscrolls itself, along the shores,
Like a book of invasions.

There goes Carlos, our Galician,
Setting alight Tech Amergin
Last night, with his mighty Pipes of Pan,
Tin whistle and libidinous grin—
And Máire Breatnach, with her violin,
Teasing it out, *The Voyage of Bran*,
Ushering autumn in.

I wish there was someone with me here
As orgy and aftermath
Give way, and Ireland reappears—
The redwood shadows of Gleann Mór
Bland as California,
And Chaplin, cut from threadbare cloth,
Our lost world-wandering myth.

I do not like this atmosphere
Where a drunk spills beer
On the calligraphy
I hide behind, like the Quiet Man.
Are these The People, staring at me?
Too dry-eyed after last night's fun—
 Nobody's father, nobody's son…

Paddy, Fíona, dearest of friends,
For a resurrected Amergin
Thank you, however it ends.
For bed and board, a B and B,
A dark flirtation, *wind off the sea*,
For blow-ins and for mythic strays,
The mornings after origin
And the shattered glass all over the place.

NAFOOEY

...the hiding-places of my power
Seem open; I approach, and then they close

Wordsworth, *The Prelude*

We fished all day, caught nothing. You were wise
Uncle Michael, dead so long ago,
With your one specimen trout, a nine-pound *ferox*
Trolled from the depths along Maumtrasna Bay,
To give up there and then.
                                   For the rest, gold weather,
Silhouettes. The boatman resting, Daddy
With a coronet of flies around his hatband,
Casting into the channel — nothing happening
But that vastness, that magnificence
All around me, entering my soul
Before I knew it. Cattle at the water,
Clattering in the shallows. The clink of a milk-can
Carrying, and the sound of a human voice,
In flat calm weather, on the tympanum
Of innocent hearing. Near and yet too far,
The big mystery, shunted into earshot,
And the long perspective into the Partry hills
That would darken slowly, on the long row home
To Ferry Bridge, and the fee for the boatman.

That, already, was a kind of death.
Past midnight, driving deeper
Into the mountains, through the twistedness of Finny,
The turfcutters' bridge, where the fish would rest
On their swims to Lough Nafooey and its greedy pike,
Its perch fry waiting to gorge themselves

On trout-spawn. Did the Hand that introduced them
Introduce evil into the universe,
Dream Nafooey? Dad had tried it once,
Got nothing, where a summer trickle entered
From the Devilsmother. It was down there somewhere
Deep in its depression, the length of it
Unseen, but weirdly felt. Poor Uncle Michael,
Daddy said, but now he is in Heaven,
And yes, I believed it.
                        For I had seen Heaven,
Felt Hell. But a day would come, returning
To that very place, when the dark would dissipate,
The bridge be just a bridge, the river a river,
The lough a ripple of innocent water
On weedy stones, and the sea an hour to the west.

THE SALMON CAGES

Padraig O'Ceidigh 1933–2008

Remember me? I was left behind
Years ago, to farm the cages.
The rest of you went away
To greater things. My friends,
My brothers, there has come a day
When you sit here, like judges,

Looking me over. The mote in the eye
Of Ireland, the suspect son
Who minds the mother, stooks the hay
In summer … boredom
And horror, the lie of the country,
Everything can be laid at my door.

Look at them, out there on the water,
Hanging, fathoms deep,
The cages. And the million selves
I might have been, ripe for the slaughter,
Dreaming continental shelves
As the factory-ship

And the ice-plant on the drizzled pier
Digest them, year by year,
Like Jonah. Ptomaine
Dropping, like a slow rain
Of pellets, into the food chain —
Tell me about it. I *live* here …

Mother is taken, once a week,
To the clinic. And John,
Arthritic from the cold of Spokane,
Is back with us now, half-witted.
The broken and the terminally sick,
We are growing again

To a kind of family. Grey days
Absorb us. The unbeautiful
Is our element—the way of duty.
No one speaks of nationhood
Anymore. There is no taste
To the fish, but sales are good.

RADIO SILENCE

Maggie Kane 1923–2018

I switch off the engine, and radio silence
Envelops me, the silence of Beat Three
In the Erriff valley, where an old oak wood,
A cut-stone bridge, were once a haven for poachers
In the witching hours. No one about
At ten o'clock on a brilliant autumn morning
With the Sheefry hills, and the Partry hills
Configured on absence, and the little sounds,
The river low on stones, after weeks of drought,
The bark, the whistle and shout, the sheep
Moving as one to the shearing-pens,
Intensifies…
                Someone is crossing over
From the old days. In an hour we will bury her
Further west, at Mullaghglass. How peaceful
It feels, neither deep in life nor death,
Outside the human airwaves, listening
As a twig falls, with the intimates, the familiars,
The ghostlife up ahead of me, remote
As small-talk over nothing — and the ghostlife
Behind me, the land of the living
Disconnected, as the vegetal world
Takes over, the eternity of the body,
Pagan, nude, abandoning itself
To water and grass, and the shooting purple vetches
Cool on the skin, the clotted cream cow parsley
Still unknown to man — and far away,
From Westport or Leenane, a car approaching.

AFTER THE BARBARIANS

Dennis O'Driscoll 1954–2012

Back then, I wanted to be
A heterosexual Cavafy—
One-night stands and office humdrum,
Speculations, over tea,
About when the barbarians might come.

A clerk with a mental age of six
Dealt with somebody's tax
In the front office. Up from the bogs
A boy as strong as an ox
Lay on his desk, did bicycle kicks

Through the whole of lunch.
Our babyfaced porter, chin double,
Filled us in on life
With his imaginary wife, called Blanche.
"She never gives me a day's trouble...."

And the ship of state plowed on,
Its lights in the Grand Canal
Reflected, myself on the telephone
Changing women, cars and flats
Or being called in, for a Friendly Chat—

And still the barbarians never came
Though the night had come
And Una given way to Joanne
On the wrecked divan ...
And now I am back from the borderlands—

There are no barbarians anymore
And maybe there never were
I have to report, to the makers of laws
Against chaos, against nothingness,
Civil servants, grey with power

Who see neither me nor their own defeat
In the sunken bicycle frames
Of the Grand Canal, at Kavanagh's Seat.
No, the barbarians never came,
Only the passing of time.

INSCAPE

Tony O'Malley 1913–2003

1

Retinal fields, horizons
Half a lifetime away,
Imprisoning sight.

Forget the crows, the death of the soul.
You are concerned, just now,
With a ground of pure perspective

That might transcend, if anything does,
The life of the little town,
The time of the little river.

Be careful, though. Remember Cézanne,
As you, a bank clerk of this parish,
Uncloset your easel…

The saint, the holy fool
Are ruined, not by violence,
Only ridicule.

2

Is it any wonder a man might get depressed
Around here? The narrow, the passionate,
Standing each other half-ones, slaking their thirsts

In the old Adelphi House, by Callan bridge
Blown up in the Civil War
Are not enough. History and hate are not enough,

Or the bringers of Independence, green paint
For the telephone boxes, moldy directories
Year upon year, stacked like Tibetan books of the dead ...

Is there an escape clause, in the social contract?
Some way through the workhouse gate
To the silence of an afterlife, in the realm of pure form,

Where the Bank, in a shower of Free State legal tender,
Washes its hands of you, and the fields await
Whoever can stand their loneliness?

3

Go, young man, to the Scilly Isles,
Go to the Bahamas.
You are, after all, only fifty.

Paint under sail, unmoor your craft
In a sailmaker's loft.
Before you reach wherever it is,

Redeem yourself, beachcomber
And driftwood, on the conflated strands
Of Nassau and Penzance,

Where everything, including the soul,
Is a found object, washed ashore,
Everyone a survivor.

So it is, when the retina strays,
When you seem to go away
And a lost Platonic world

Comes back to you—Kilkenny, Callan,
Ireland itself, the mote in the eye
Dissolving as you die.

PART THREE

i.m. Mary Bridget McKavanagh Madden

1925–2014

THE FELLING

1

There was talk of cutting down the pine trees.
For years it went on. One day, it happened.
And I came back, like rain on the wind,

From a great elsewhere, to the ruined Parthenon
Of trunks, the raped Arcadian grove
Once picnicked in by sisters, maiden aunts

Now shades of themselves, the lake shining through
In the distance, spread like a water table
With its own best silver. Death in the air,

A smell of resin, sweetness given off
By trees and women — innocence grown old
Without corruption. Growth rings, in the yellow

Crosscut flesh of logs in the yard,
Circles within circles, closed,
Inscrutable now, whatever their wisdom was.

2

I lift one onto the fire, and listen for the wind.
Yes, but without the trees. That deep roar
To stand in the yard and hearken to, at night,

A whisky in hand, a blaze of constellations
Above me, and quarreling waterfowl
Out by the foreshore ... All the sounds that carry

And are lost. Stray love-cars, snuffed-out light,
Gropings in the dark, old generations.
Red traces in the morning. Genuflectings

Into the Eighties. Duty, never ease,
A life on both knees, a blowback of wood-ash,
Pre-decease … I hear it now, the wind,

And sit alone, at the heart of a crime
I never witnessed. Everything will change —
New names, new faces. Yes, but without the trees.

3

They grow and they grow, and then the soil thins,
The roots die out. They were all about shadow
On hot days, a windbreak in winter,

A ghostlife, right through sleep. But physical, there,
Real presences, second selves put out
To wind and weather. Suddenly, one day,

A man appeared, to measure length of shade.
I can hear it yet, the buzz and snarl
Of chainsaw, the soft crash of the upper boughs

Into the dreaming mind, and the fine dry smoke
That hangs in the air a little while
And is gone. New silence, static time,

Lobotomized and vacuous, staring out
From the inside of a shaven head, a house
With its windows wide on strange horizons.

4

Hetty is dying, above in her room.
The hewer of wood, the drawer of water. Work
Has ceased about the place. An air of waiting,

Memories... Antoinette, whose man proved violent.
Jess, who was betrayed. Elizabeth, Nan,
Who never married. Cissy, in America

Fifty years. Her grave in the Middle West.
Listen, creaks and groans. A sisterhood
Of old trees, leaning into each other,

Conspiratorial, whispering on every wind
The inside story... I have strayed
Into their circle. Dead, they stare at me,

Offer me cakes, cold tea, a place at a distance
From the human family. Arcadians,
Darkened by their own indigenous shadow.

5

Now I see another shore, in the distance,
Hacked free, in treeless space. A dream,
Unearthly. God knows what the garden seeds—

Arum lilies shooting into existence
Ages later, to amaze us, now,
With all they sowed, the lost ones. Stewardship,

Not ownership. An entering into possession
Of life after death. A future flattened out,
And now eternally present. Lines of descent

No longer flesh, but spirit. Through the barred trunks
A new, a far perspective, out of time.
Goodbye dears, and thank you. Everything

Has run wild again, but nothing is lost.
I stand in the long grass. Arcadia, Parthenon—
Everything that shadowed us has gone.

IN BRONTË COUNTRY

To the young minister, who enters
Without knowing it, a Brontë novel,
Marriage will seem like nothing on earth.

Religion could never prepare him
For the dripping wet days, the wind in the flue,
The huge Atlantic

Men, dismasted, breathe their last in—
The distillations of time,
The mists at the windowpane, rubbed clear

Of visibility, into vision.
Where, he may ask, are space and time
When the ruined farm is one with the parsonage,

Ashes glow for centuries
In the grate, and the crewel-work
Of narrative, the hemistich of rhyme

Keep a sisterhood warm?
The bun in the oven, life to come,
Will never be taken out in time,

And the rest, dead women,
Is history, cold in the hall,
Unspoken, when the wise woman calls.

SPINSTERS

In the literal sense
They wielded needles,

Knitted, sewed.
Hence the name, and hence

The spinning of yarns,
For words, too, were involved,

The warp and woof
Of narrative, through time

And generation ... Spinsters?
Mothers mostly, sharing

With their own daughters
Good and bad, between themselves

And the four walls—
And nothing too small

To be held to the light
Like thread, and moistened

With a wet tongue, passed
Through an infinitesimal eye

To a paradise
Of vestments, wedding dresses,

Christening robes and epic tales
Where the hero,

The heroine, stood in the way
Of real time, every day.

NOTES FOR A TOWNLAND

The men are silent workers,
The women never stop talking.

The kitchens are blast furnaces
Of breadmaking. Outside,

The cold is hard, material—
Iron for the soul. And the yards

Concrete, the problems real.
A woman can vulcanize a tire

And still be a ball of fire. Two elders
Take in a love-child. All solutions

Arrive with time, since life,
Which is bigger than everyone,

Must be believed in. Religion?
Yes, in the outward sense—

Observances, liturgies—
But mainly a crowding together

Once a week, against death
Which never hides itself

But is there, on the hill
Behind the church, the hill of crosses,

Like a third party, to the silent men,
The endlessly talking women.

HONESTY

This, then, is the famous flower
Called Honesty, translucent
In death, and not to be confused
With the usual vetches, heirs apparent
Earth throws over itself
Like purple patches.
                    It took a hand,
A woman's hand, to plant it here
By a field-gate, in a tumbledown yard
Far gone on the path to nothingness.
Who will come afterwards, foot in the door
Half-open, till I hear him out?
There was once a house here he will say,
Holding it up, the original key,
And now it belongs to me.
                    Grasses, weeds—
The rearguard action of the defenseless
Against time. Nasturtiums
You could eat at a pinch, make tea from,
And buckets of pinks, potato-flowers,
A wild cornucopia, crowding
At a deserted window.
Mother and daughter, sister and wife,
Will it be held against me
In the grave, like a sprig of Honesty—
My seen-through interloper's life?

THE DECOYS

He stepped into the water and steadily began
to walk. He took one step more, and vanished.

Deirdre Madden, *The Birds of the Innocent Wood*

He got to where the decoys were hidden
Below high water mark
Between two alders and a waterlogged punt.

Six of them, stuffed
In a hollow. Fake mallard, lost to the hunt
For all those things that only come unbidden—

Never dead because never alive
Except on first impression.
Was there no world to go back to anymore

Through the treeline, and the disinherited fields,
The fool's gold of an afternoon's light,
A house without succession?

He would be lost for a while, then found,
Having stripped himself of everything and drowned
In the name of art, and left behind him

Wooden decoys, six in all,
Afloat on the water, and a mating call
That brought the creatures in before the Fall.

THE SWEEP

Everything was thirty years ago
Including the last time the chimneysweep
Put in an appearance. Birds have built
In the choked windpipe
Of the lumb. The coke-fumes
In the bedroom, smokeless guilt
Invisible as eye-motes, slowly make themselves felt.

Spread the dust-sheet now, on thirty years,
And start the vacuum up.
Stand back, while the nests of blood
Aborted, and the unborn generations
Disappear into the sack
Of darkness with a sigh
And the hearth is cold, and you can see the sky.

JERICHO

Milking-parlors, blue-lit snow—
Once they called it Jericho.

A derivation from Old Irish
Or a bulldozed parish

God's own people starved in, sinned.
Whether or which, they are farming the wind

Up there, on Henry Gribbin's lands,
On Genevieve's at the Manse,

And catching the breath of heaven.
Fields of green-gold, interwoven

Like vestments, with corn-sheaves, grapes,
Fall from the hand of Apocalypse

As Ginny, age-old sewer of shrouds
And coronation robes, drops dead

In the last house left on Staffordstown Road.
One kind of myth has been exploded,

One kind of clock has ceased to tick.
The barefoot girls of Moneynick

Dressed in flour-bags, sugar-bags
Schoolgirls once, are spinsters, hags,

Old wives' tales from Jericho.
For marrying in, for needing to know,

For crossing the strangest of borders
Friend, you'd get less for murder

They tell me, as I show
My hand too openly, and Jericho

Gives up its ghost to the loud bulldozer,
And never be any the wiser.

THE PLACE OF THE STONINGS

Knockloghrim 1969

Here the accounts diverge. The written word
Can only go so far, before dissolving
In grey apocryphal haze.... And the dead are no help

Who came that day through the trees, and saw the mountains
Spread before them, like a lost ideal
They were singing of—the marchers and stewards

Coming, ever so slowly, round the bend,
To be stoned, descended on
By God's right hand, His eggs in a single basket,

Before vanishing, who had given up on themselves
Long ago, into an image of justice,
A future where the trees, the road remain,

And fifty years go by, empty of anything
But gossip at a crossroads,
Feathergrass singing, mountains lost in rain.

THE PURE SOURCE

Beware of the pure source

Edward Said

Maura, Frank, myself and Paddy McCloskey
With his 150,000 salmon roe,
His marl and gravel for the man-made flow
Are interfering with nature
For its own good, sloshing about
In the shallows, where the hen-fish wallow
Steadying themselves, on tail and fin,
As the little males move in,
The gigolos, in their red striped livery,
Who never go to sea.
                    We are not alone
Up here, beyond our comfort zone,
Dungiven miles below us, and the lights of Kilrea—
A no-man's-land, adventured into
By lost souls, and the ghosts of the IRA.

Eyes are watching, from the barn owl's tree,
The otter's holt, by the hatchery.

Another shadow joins us. Why, I wonder,
Are we poking about after dark
On a pitch-black winter night of supernovae,
Constellations, Milky Way…?
Night vision, I hear him say,
For what swims beneath our own reflection.
Paddy makes a joke about gender,
No one laughs. It is late, too late
For all of that—for Frank with his photographs
That will never come out,

And Maura, with a miner's lamp
On her forehead, and me without gloves,
Dreaming hot toddy and lemon, honey and cloves ...

Only the shadow, with his infinite patience
Beyond fish-kill, future of nation,
Slurry-pit of civilization,
Flushes still, in deep December,
Guns and bootleg whiskey, organizations
Of which he was once a member.

DIATOMITE

The fossilized plankton
Of an Ice Age sea
Beneath Lough Neagh. White coal
That comes away in lumps

From the earth-face. Like a sheet,
The glacial tide drew back
For millions of years,
Exposing us, beachcombers

Of our own dried structures,
Killing-grounds. No question
Of vein or seam
Or a lost community

Sold out to the business ethic.
We who survive it
Remember its use—
Explosives and cosmetics.

THE ULSTER CYCLE

To be paid in land and cattle
Like the first poets, is all
I would ask, as the combine harvester
Bucks and rattles

Downfield, into deep July,
The pair of us chatting, Conor and I,
Our John Deere riding shotgun
With a neighbor's Massey Ferguson.

Which is worse, the epidemic
Of writing schools, or the pseudo-poetry
Of agro-economics?
Swallowed in immediacy

He ignores me, and concentrates,
Adjusting his right-hand lever
As the arm swings over
And a green ejaculate

Streams into the trailer.
Off it sways, from its pas de deux,
Another Massey sways into view,
Another perfect neighbor.

Who am I to be putting my oar in—
I, with my paper qualifications,
He with his scattering of farms
Going back for generations

Into the hinterlands, and the heights
Behind Lough Neagh—*the uncles, in-laws,*
None, for all their grazing rights,
Able to read or write—

And the day between us, Conor and I,
Charioteers of the Ulster Cycle,
His the manic concentration,
Mine the lazy eye

On the jump-seat, looking away
Past Mallon's acres, land and cattle,
Into the myth, the heart of the matter—
Dreaming, you might say.

TOOME

Poor in everything
But water. Unconsecrated,
Not yet changed to wine,
I made it mine,

Where time condenses
Into years
And a heartspace clears
Between nothing and nothing.

I entered it long ago
Like a monastery—
Stayed … A novice
Not of holy rite,

But an eremite
Of poetry. Thrown back
Among outcasts, pariahs,
Making my soul

At a waiting-place,
A ford. Indwelling
Years on end, in a single cell,
Under a bare lightbulb,

Bibles, dusty breviaries
My companions. To the west
The Sperrins, to the east
A glow of townships

In the darkness. Lorries, cars,
A world on the move—
Not here, among spirits,
A widowed sisterhood

Glimpsing, in blown smidgens
Of rain, indigenous skies
On a windowpane, epiphanies
Older than religion.

GERMINAL

The heavy harrowing
First, and then the light.

The breaking down of clay
Into fine tilth, and the tractor,

Soundtrack to an August day,
Flattening whole acres

As it rattles around —
The slurry-spreader, stone-breaker.

Only from unearthly height
Does it make sense —

The circles, figures of eight
The Massey Ferguson half-creates,

And me as usual, alienated,
Sitting on the fence.

2

Round he comes again,
Hugh Carey. Shooting rights

And two grass crops a year
And the whole place his, by sheer default,

Though not for half a century yet.
Meanwhile in they go, his salts

Of phosphate, and his coatings of lime
On darkness, primary matter,

The pair of us its stewards
In and out of time,

Each, in the eye of the Almighty
The other's looking-glass,

One the holy meaningless,
One the flesh as grass.

3

Tiny as a fleck
And next to nothing, the grass-seed

In his palm. *A dry bed
And a wet blanket would be luck*

Hugh says, meaning rain.
The widow who owns the place

Looks about her and dies.
The widower takes to wife again,

The heavy harrowing goes on
And the light, as I sit and wait

And pray to the Almighty
For mustard seed, devoid of mass,

Too infinitely small for grass,
Unreal, to germinate.

PRAEGER

Robert Lloyd Praeger 1865–1953

Before and after the age of borders,
With the Ordovician, the Carboniferous layers
Of the Sperrins (where else could you stand

So far back from Ireland, and still be in Ireland)
East to west, not north to south,
You go about searching for the edible, the medicinal,

In a single berry. Sleeping in henhouses,
Feet sticking out through the window, roosters perched
On your boots, announcing the times to come.

Huge is the shade of uprightness, through the days
Forgotten now, in the forgotten mountains
Where a Field Club spreading out, in health and innocence

Calls to itself and fades, in a wilderness of stars
Winking like space stations, dissolving like a drone
Supersonic, into silence, lintels of smashed stone,

Abandoned valleys, grass of oblivion
Grown again over everything—and that single berry
Ireland obfuscates, your great unknown.

THE EARLIEST BREAKFAST
IN NORTHERN IRELAND

It has to do with cold iron. Which, in turn,
Has to do with necessity. It has to do
With winters and long distances, and the juggernauts

Of haulage, already too late, no matter how early,
For the great day dawning, away in the east
Or call it Belfast, towards which they endlessly travel

On an Ulster fried breakfast, out of whatever night.
It has to do with ice and undercarriage,
Untouchable, lest the hand anneal forever

To that particular metal. It has to do
With biting on bullets, and the taste of the machine
In coffee and tea, and the Sperrins behind

And Belfast up ahead
Still getting out of bed. And the notional countryside
All around, shot through like darkness

With the light of limited understanding,
Peripheral vision, as Northern Ireland comes awake,
Gable by whitewashed gable

Writ with Scripture. Six-lane highways,
Narrowings into tunnels, huge hydraulic hiss,
The carriage of heavy goods, drawn level with each other

In bible time, as breakfast settles down
Between Randalstown and Glengormley, creation
And apocalypse, and everything converges.

AT THE GRAVE OF SEAMUS HEANEY

Bellaghy churchyard, County Derry

Because I know the territory
And have lived here
All these years, by my own lights,

I let myself in by rights
But carefully, lest my presence
Breed disquiet.

A raised catafalque
Of clay, a chain-link fence
Your self-defense

From the living shadow
Of the dispossessed,
The critic in the long grass

Of Arcadia. Birds in a bush,
The twittering mesh
Of the inarticulate

In mist-nets, skeins
Of language, brought to hand
In no-man's-land … For your pains,

Thank you. And for leaving me,
This side of the grave,
Lough Neagh, my Land under Wave,

The Toome shore
And the yet-to-be-explored
Immensities of Doss,

The burning glass
Of water widening to a lens
Or a loss of innocence —

Love-cars, Sunday afternoons,
Too much knowledge, much too soon,
The knowledge of death

Behind the senses,
Knowledge stripped of all that myth
Of hope and history, future tenses —

Acid jazz, the concrete bulk
And small-hours nightclub razzmatazz
That is still The Elk,

The haulage thundering east and west
In juggernauts of driven power
And spiritual exhaust…

"When Master Pollock's bagpipes play
Outside, it must be rain."
Maybe once, but not again

In the drinking-dens
Of Cranfield, Grange and Moneyglass
And the sheep-pens

High in the Sperrins, rattling tin
As a ghost might rattle a door,
Invite himself back in

To the middle ground
Of Ulster, the daily round
This Monday morning, no one about,

Where time to spare,
A one-sided conversation
With the dead, is mine to share,

Who have been everywhere
But home, with the fleshers,
Eelmen, buried here,

The cattle doctors, way back when,
The Scullions, the Lavertys,
The haulier MacErlean,

The Heaneys, Devlins, set in stone,
The local names, to whom, one day,
I just may add my own.